Original title:
Solar System Shenanigans

Copyright © 2025 Creative Arts Management OÜ
All rights reserved.

Author: Isabella Rosemont
ISBN HARDBACK: 978-1-80567-855-7
ISBN PAPERBACK: 978-1-80567-976-9

Whimsical Worlds

In a place where moons dance with glee,
Jupiter spins tea cups for free.
Uranus chuckles, oh what a sight,
As Saturn's rings twirl in delight.

Venus plays hide and seek with Mars,
While comets zoom past, wishing on stars.
Neptune juggles bubbles with flair,
And Pluto grins, though he's not quite there.

Celestial Frolics

Mercury's racing, just like a blur,
While Venus tries on a new purple fur.
Mars is painting the sky bright red,
While Earth plays hopscotch, laughing instead.

Saturn throws parties with rings made of glow,
And asteroids join in, dancing to show.
Jupiter's giant, but timid and shy,
While the Sun beams down with a wink from the sky.

Stellar Silliness

A black hole sneezed, and oh what a mess,
It swallowed some stars, which caused quite distress.
But laughter erupted in cosmic delight,
As giants made jokes that echoed in night.

Tiny meteors raced, but never could win,
While space-time giggled, creating a spin.
Alien critters played tag with a flare,
And danced on the rings with not a single care.

Alien Amusements

With purple polka dots and a twist of lime,
Aliens held a grand joke-telling time.
They tickled the stars until they would shine,
And puzzled the planets with riddles divine.

Mars wore a tutu, oh what a sight,
While Earth spun around in sheer delight.
Galaxies giggled from far and near,
As space echoed laughter, a cosmic cheer!

Planetary Pranks

Mercury's fast, it always zooms,
Jupiter's storms burst like balloons.
Earth forgets to water the trees,
While Mars giggles in the breeze.

Venus wears a veil so thick,
Neptune's waves play a cheeky trick.
Uranus rolls, a silly sight,
Caught in giggles, day and night.

Orbital Oddities

Pluto waves with a tiny grin,
While comets are chasing, they spin.
Asteroids party, music loud,
Rockets join in, feeling proud.

Starry skies twinkle with glee,
Constellations dance, wild and free.
Black holes yawn, give a big sigh,
While space dust winks as they fly.

Galactic Guffaws

Saturn laughs, its rings in a twirl,
Mars tells jokes that make stars swirl.
Comets jump in a comical race,
While meteors fall with a silly face.

The Milky Way giggles along,
With cosmic tunes, a playful song.
Galaxies spin, what a sight!
All in fun, through day and night.

Saturn's Silly Rings

Saturn spins with flair and style,
Its rings dance round, making us smile.
Neighbors peek and come to see,
What fun awaits in the cosmic spree.

Jupiter jests, its clouds are bold,
While funny craters stories are told.
Uranus chuckles, a cheeky breeze,
As stars all twinkle with giggles and tease.

Orbiting Oddities

In the dance of cosmic cheer,
Planets twirl without a fear.
Jupiter's storms spin like a top,
While Saturn's rings just never stop.

Uranus rolls on its side,
With a tilt that gives it pride.
Mars plays tag with little moons,
While Venus hums her funny tunes.

Saturn's Silly Symphony

Saturn strums on rings of ice,
Each note is silly, oh so nice.
Comets join in for a laugh,
As asteroids dance on a giraffe.

Neptune serenades the night,
With bubbles that twinkle bright.
Pluto joins with a shy grin,
Singing softly, let's begin!

Venusian Vexations

Venus throws a cosmic fit,
Cloudy moods, but doesn't quit.
She swirls around with cheeky flair,
Making martians stop and stare.

With volcanoes that just won't sleep,
She stirs the night, a lively sweep.
Her dances spark a fiery glow,
While Earthlings ponder, 'Is it a show?'

Mercury's Magical Mayhem

Mercury whizzes, fast and bright,
Chasing shadows, what a sight!
He zips past Venus on a dare,
Like a mischievous little flare.

Bouncing 'round the Sun with glee,
He plays tag with a solar sea.
His shenanigans, oh what a tease,
Bringing laughter, shooting stars with ease.

Jupiter's Jovial Jests

Jupiter giggles as he spins,
His Great Red Spot holds all the wins.
Clouds swirl in a riot of hues,
While moons play cards, exchanging their blues.

Saturn snickers with rings so wide,
Her laughter echoes, a cosmic tide.
While comets crash the jovial scene,
Sprinkling stardust, a glimmering sheen.

Interstellar Escapades

Mars tried dancing, he tripped on dust,
Venus just giggled, her smile a must.
Mercury zips with a wink and a cheer,
While Neptune just laughs, "Get over here!"

Pluto's debate on being a star,
"Am I too small? Do I travel far?"
Everyone chuckles, it's all in good fun,
As space-time tickles under a glowing sun.

Moonlit Mischief

Under the gaze of a silvery glow,
The Moon throws a party, putting on a show.
Stars bring confetti, sparkles galore,
While asteroids bust moves on a cosmic floor.

Lunar laughter rolls 'round like a song,
As meteors dance, not caring for wrong.
They twirl and they spin, with glee in their eyes,
In the grand cosmic ball, beneath starry skies.

Comet's Comedic Tail

A comet zoomed by with a wink and a tail,
Leaving behind a sparkly trail.
"Catch me if you can!" it cheekily cried,
While planets burst out laughing, filled with pride.

Venus threw glitter, and Earth joined the race,
Cheerful chaos in this silly space.
As the comet danced, swirling through night,
Galaxies snorted, what a joyful sight!

Dance of the Distant Worlds

Jupiter twirls, with a gas-filled grin,
While tiny Pluto tries to jump in.
Saturn's rings spin in a merry swirl,
While Mars just laughs, oh what a whirl!

Venus winks, her clouds all hazy,
Mercury zooms, feeling quite crazy.
Earth does the moonwalk, oh what a sight,
As comets giggle, dancing through the night.

Cosmic Laughter Leaves.

Neptune's blues play a silly song,
While asteroids bop along all day long.
Uranus spins, with a tilt and a shout,
While meteors race, trying not to pout.

Shooting stars wink, with wishes to share,
Mars jokes about having too much air.
Sun laughs bright, as shadows chase,
In this vast void, there's always space.

Galactic Giggles

Stars explode with a chuckle or two,
While comets make trails, shiny and new.
Black holes twirl, like they're spinning tops,
And little moons play leapfrog, never stops.

Rings of Saturn swing like a fun fair ride,
While Martians hide, then peek with pride.
The Milky Way tickles, with stardust delight,
A universal giggle in the vast moonlight.

Cosmic Carnival

Galactic swings twirl from here to there,
While Jupiter shouts, 'Can you find my hair?'
Neptune's carousel goes round and round,
As moons join in, laughter is found.

Saturn's booth sells rings made of laugh,
Venus giggles, she's always the gaff.
Together they frolic, in patterns so grand,
In this cosmic fair, hand in hand.

Nebula Nonsense

In a cloud of colors bright,
Stars play hide and seek at night.
Jupiter's got a silly grin,
While Saturn spins in a hula spin.

Uranus jokes with a cheeky wink,
Pluto pops up, just to think.
With a burst, the colors swirl,
Galactic giggles make them twirl.

Celestial Capers

Mercury races, fast as a bolt,
Venus laughs as her charms jolt.
Mars in red is painting a scene,
While Earth rolls by, like a sparkling bean.

Neptune sighs with a watery glee,
As comets dance and laugh with glee.
A cosmic circus up high and far,
With glittering planets as the stars.

Asteroid Antics

Asteroids tumble with giggling sounds,
Bouncing around like playful hounds.
One trips and calls for a cosmic mate,
While others laugh, "Now isn't that great?"

They juggle moons with a wobbling flair,
Then chase some sunlight without a care.
Space rocks rolling in a grand parade,
Chasing the comet that's coming to trade.

Lunar Larks

The Moon's throwing parties, it's quite a sight,
With cheese for snacks, oh what a delight.
Lunar bunnies hop around the crater,
While shooting stars writhe as the creator.

They play tag with the shadows, so sly and spry,
Crafting constellations that shimmer and fly.
In the night, their laughter rings,
As the universe dances and joyously sings.

Celestial Revels

The sun wore shades, so bright and bold,
While Mercury danced, feeling oh so cold.
Venus tried baking, but burnt the pie,
And Mars just chuckled, giving it a try.

Jupiter's storm made quite the mess,
While Saturn's rings sparked fashion stress.
Uranus rolled laughter in its blue haze,
While Neptune hummed tunes in strange, funky ways.

Planetary Parody

Earth threw a party, invited the crew,
With space snacks and drinks, a cosmic brew.
But Pluto got jealous, said, "Wait, hold on!"
"Why am I not listed in this fun song?"

Mars showed up with a space rover ride,
But tripped on a crater and fell to the side.
Jupiter laughed, spilled gas in the air,
Saying, "Next time, wear boots, it's only fair!"

Comet's Comedic Chase

A comet zoomed past with a giggling tail,
Chasing the stars with an endless wail.
It tickled a planet, who started to shake,
While asteroids laughed at the pranks it could make.

"Catch me if you can!" the comet did shout,
As moons spun around, filled with joyful doubt.
Light-years weren't long when you're having a blast,
Turning cosmic races into memories vast.

Jovial Journey Through Space

On a spaceship made of candy and goo,
The crew was all jesters, just passing through.
They juggled the stars and danced in the void,
Tickling black holes, the fun they enjoyed.

Gravity giggled as they floated around,
Riding moonbeams, no limits were found.
With laughter in orbit, they spun through the night,
Creating a carnival of cosmic delight.

Jovian Joyride

A giant storm with winds that spin,
The clouds are laughing, where to begin?
Jupiter's moons all dance in a line,
Saturn's rings sparkle, oh what a sign!

Mars took a trip on a comet's back,
He's showing off his rusty red crack!
With a wink and a nudge, oh what a sight,
That little planet loves a good flight!

Venus is sulking, too hot to play,
But Mercury zooms, it's a dizzy display.
He races the sun, oh what a thrill,
While Pluto waits, sighing, "What a chill!"

The stars giggle softly, watching it all,
As comets play tag, having a ball.
In this great expanse, laughter is king,
Each planet brings joy, let the fun ring!

Celestial Capers in the Cosmos

Neptune's got a whirlpool, spins real fast,
He dips and twirls, a cosmic dance blast.
Uranus chuckles, winks with a grin,
"I'll join your party, let the fun begin!"

Earth's throwing confetti, look at it fly,
While the Moon ciphers jokes, oh my oh my!
Mars is now juggling with moons on a dare,
And Venus is painting, spreading good flair!

A meteor shower, oh what a show,
Shooting stars lighting up, row by row.
Mercury spins, he loves to tease,
While aliens join in with dance moves that please!

In this cosmic circus, we giggle and cheer,
With laughter and light, it's the best atmosphere.
From gas giants to rocks, each plays their part,
In this vast universe, we share from the heart!

Cosmic Revelry

The moon threw a party, stars danced in delight,
Jupiter spilled juice, what a silly sight!
Mars wore a hat, Venus twirled around,
In this merry chaos, laughter's all around.

Saturn played music, rings shaking with glee,
Pluto showed up late, sipping iced tea.
Asteroids were juggling, comets joined in,
Galactic giggles echoed, let the fun begin!

Planetary Positivity

Earth baked a cake, frosted with clouds,
Mercury brought cupcakes, drawing in crowds.
Neptune did the limbo, so low it went,
While Mars cracked jokes, here's what he meant!

Uranus wore shades, said 'I'm too cool!'
Saturn spun round, breaking all the rules.
With laughter aloft and smiles on their face,
Each planet felt bright in this cosmic place.

Astrological Amusements

The sun made a joke that burned with a flare,
And the stars rolled their twinkling eyes in despair.
Mercury raced swiftly, tripped on a beam,
While Pluto just chuckled, all part of the dream.

Neptune splashed water, a whimsical play,
Asteroids winked cheerfully, throwing confetti all day.
In this cosmic circus, everyone beams,
As laughter ignites our most starry dreams.

Twilight Tumbles

As dusk painted skies with colors so bright,
Planets took chances, avoiding the night.
Earth fell in giggles, rolled down a hill,
While Luna spun softly, a dance to thrill.

With telescopes ready, they gazed up above,
Stars winking down, like they're in love.
Galaxies twirled, uniting in fun,
In the realm of twilight, laughter's never done!

Lunar Laughter

The moon played tricks with a shiny grin,
Tossed comets like confetti, let the fun begin.
Stars giggled softly, danced in the night,
While planets all juggled, what a silly sight!

Mars wore a tutu, red and bright,
While Venus baked cookies, a starry delight.
Jupiter spun plates, a circus in space,
Oh what a party, in this cosmic place!

Whimsical Wanderings Among the Stars

In cosmic cafes, snacks float around,
Saturn sipped ice cream, without making a sound.
Pluto played tag with a comet so fast,
While our dear Earth chuckled, holding on to the past.

Neptune wore glasses, looked wise and sage,
As stars shared their stories, setting the stage.
Uranus cracked jokes, slightly offbeat,
While all of us laughed at the strange cosmic feat!

Astral Antics

A mischievous meteor zipped by with flair,
Tickling the tails of all who were there.
Mars did the limbo, quite low to the ground,
While Earth spun around, with laughter profound.

Asteroids swung like bells in the breeze,
Making the galaxy giggle with ease.
From Venus to Mercury, all had a ball,
In this cosmic carnival, the best one of all!

Timeless Tumbles

A time-traveling star took a tumble so grand,
Spilling stardust and giggles all over the land.
Mercury raced by, said, 'Catch me if you dare,'
While cosmic confetti flew out in the air.

With light years of laughter, they swirled and they spun,
An interstellar circus, oh what joyous fun!
Astronauts in costumes twirled with delight,
In this dance of the cosmos, they shone ever bright!

The Asteroid Adventure

In the belt where rocks collide,
Asteroids race with glee,
One hit a comet's tail,
And danced in zero gravity.

They twirled like goofy dancers,
Playing dodgeball with the sun,
One bonked a planet's nose,
And giggled—oh, what fun!

But watch out for those orbits,
They're wild and full of cheer,
One misstep might send you flying,
To Pluto's icy sphere!

So buckle up, dear stargazers,
For this ride's a cosmic blast,
With asteroids playing tag,
And memories meant to last!

Shooting Stars Shuffling

Look at those stars shooting by,
With tails of sparkling light,
They're not just wishing on dreams,
But playing hide and seek at night!

One star took a sneaky dive,
Right into a cosmic pool,
Splashing stardust all around,
Making the galaxy drool!

They shuffle and skip in their dance,
While winking at the moon,
Crafting wishes with their trails,
A whimsical tune to croon.

So when you see them flicker,
Just know they're out for fun,
With a giggle and a twinkle,
Their endless joy's begun!

Celestial Shenanigans

Up in the sky where planets play,
They share a cosmic joke,
Venus teased Mars today,
With a funny little poke.

Saturn's rings are hula hoops,
That dance around its waist,
And Jupiter's great red spot,
Is just a clumsy face!

Neptune whirls in watery blues,
Making silly bubble sounds,
While Mercury zooms past all,
With rapid, speedy bounds.

Together they spin and laugh,
A galaxy of cheer,
Creating joy in starlit paths,
For all the world to hear!

The Mischievous Moons

Oh, the moons are such pranksters,
They love a game of hide and seek,
With Jupiter's moons sneaking up,
And making Saturn's rings squeak!

One moon stole a shadow,
And wore it as a hat,
While another tried to jump rope,
With space dust flat!

They giggle and spin around,
Creating orbits of delight,
While chasing the sun's warm rays,
In the dark of starry night.

So if you hear a cosmic laugh,
Don't think it's just a tale,
It's those crafty little moons,
On their merry little trail!

Celestial Chuckles

In the sky, stars giggle bright,
Mars just dropped his favorite kite.
Jupiter's moons play hide and seek,
While Mercury's always late to speak.

Venus steals the sun with flair,
Saturn's rings twirl through the air.
Pluto shouts, "I'm still the best!"
But the dwarf planet needs a rest.

Neptune's waves crash with a jest,
Uranus laughs, he knows no rest.
Through the cosmos, laughter flies,
As asteroids dance in the skies.

In this realm of wacky glee,
Aliens toast with cups of tea.
Through the years, they share their cheer,
A universe where jokes are dear.

Orbital Oddities

Mercury zooms, never a break,
His speed's enough to cause a quake.
Venus winks, what a bright star!
Turns out she's really a pop star.

Earth rolls by with a laugh so loud,
While Mars grins, pretending to be proud.
Jupiter's storms dance a wild jig,
As Saturn simply does a big wig.

Uranus spins quite askew,
Whispering secrets to its crew.
Neptune's trident causes a splash,
While comets zoom by in a flash.

Rings and moons all join the fun,
Dancing beneath a cosmic sun.
Stars shoot jokes across the sky,
In this world, laughter will never die.

Comet's Caprices

A comet dashed with a silly grin,
Leaving trails where mischief begins.
Asteroids chase like dogs in play,
Bumping into each without delay.

Mars pops popcorn under a tree,
While Venus tries to sing off-key.
Jupiter chuckles, his belly shakes,
As Saturn spins, "Oh! Earthquake!"

Pluto makes up a funny rhyme,
Though he insists he's still prime time.
Neptune plots a prank on the sun,
Laughter echoes, oh what fun!

Galaxies swirl, the antics soar,
In this vastness, there's always more.
With every twist and every turn,
The cosmos smiles, sharing its humor to learn.

Spacetime Shenanigans

Space-time antics all around,
With laughter, joy, and silly sound.
Light years travel on a slide,
As planets join in for the ride.

Venus cracks jokes from high above,
While Mars giggles at the stars he loves.
Mercury races, trying to win,
But he trips and spins in a dizzy spin.

Saturn's rings spin tight and fast,
Creating halos that just won't last.
Uranus cracks a cosmic pun,
As galaxies twirl, oh what fun!

With rocket ships and goofy beams,
Through the void, we chase our dreams.
Orbiting joy in a universe bright,
Living for laughter, day and night.

Quasar Quirks

In the galaxy's bright glow, they play,
Stars spin in their wacky ballet.
One comet trips, with a sparkle and crash,
While planets giggle, in a colorful flash.

A black hole whispers its spooky jokes,
While meteors dance like silly folks.
With each supernova, a party erupts,
As stardust sprinkles, and laughter corrupts.

Planets in pajamas, just having a ball,
Racing each other, but who'll take the fall?
Asteroids bouncing, a cosmic dodgeball,
In this swirling chaos, there's fun for all.

Astrological Antics

The moon pulls pranks, lighting dim caves,
While Venus slips on its shiny waves.
Mars tells jokes that make folks shout,
As Saturn's rings twirl, no doubt about.

Jupiter laughs, with its stormy face,
Throwing gas clouds in a funny race.
Mercury zips, moving way too fast,
Making all the stars question, 'Will he last?'

But oh, dear Pluto, the tiny prankster,
Cracks wise with comets, always a jester.
Amongst the chaos and stellar delight,
Cosmic antics take flight, oh what a sight!

Comedic Constellations

Orion's belt is a fashion faux pas,
With sausages hanging, oh what a draw!
Ursa Major just can't find her way,
While shooting stars giggle, 'It's time to play!'

Cassiopeia strikes a ridiculous pose,
While Leo's mane gives out silly woes.
Cygnus the swan can't stop doing the twist,
As Andromeda dances, too cute to resist!

With every twinkle, they share their best,
Laughter erupts, they're humor-obsessed.
In this vast sky, where giggles ignite,
Each constellation's a comedy night!

Orbiting Oddball Adventures

In a spaceship spun of candy and dreams,
The crew of oddballs all plot silly schemes.
Venus hoards snacks, with a laugh and a grin,
While Mars bakes cookies in a fluffy tin.

Neptune holds bubbles that never pop,
And Saturn rolls hula hoops nonstop.
Uranus swings by, just to say hi,
'Hey folks, let's soar through the blueberry sky!'

Gathering stardust for a galactic feast,
Comets join hands, their laughter increased.
As they zoom and whirl in a cosmic ride,
Every adventure is filled with joy and pride.

Nebula Nonsense

In a cloud of color, stars play hide and seek,
While comets zoom by, giving quite the squeak.
Planets spin round like a merry-go-round,
Laughing at gravity, they're joyously unbound.

Tiny moons chuckle with a whimsical grin,
Twinkling and winking, they're always in.
Galaxies whirl with a twinkly dance,
Inviting the universe to join in the prance.

Asteroids break out in a rock-and-roll tune,
Grooving through space, chasing the moon.
Black holes chuckle, "We're the life of the show!"
Swallowing stardust and throwing confetti below.

So when you gaze up at the starry expanse,
Remember the fun of the cosmic romance.
In the heart of the cosmos, laughter is grand,
As we all join in this stellar band.

Martian Mayhem

On the red planet, where dust storms erupt,
Martians play pranks without a hiccup.
They dangle their antennas, tickle each ear,
Chasing each other for a round of career.

Rockets zoom past with a giggle and cheer,
As aliens bicker on who drives the steer.
With tiny green hands, they throw soft space pies,
Laughing and rolling under Martian skies.

Jupiter's folks peek through Martian windows,
Wondering what kind of trouble time bends.
"Oh, let's build forts with moon rocks galore!"
Giggling loudly as they secure each door.

In a lively corner of the cosmos' expanse,
Where Martian mayhem gives laughter a chance.
Floating on cliffs made of strawberry jam,
Schematic delight in their whimsical plan.

Cosmic Carnival

Step right up to the great cosmic fair,
With starry rides that float through the air.
Saturn spins plates with a dazzling flair,
While Uranus juggles in a giggly pair.

Space creatures dance on a comet's bright tail,
With candy-striped rockets, they set off to sail.
Shooting star fireworks go pop in the night,
Lighting up faces with pure, gleeful delight.

Astrophysical games, their favorite affair,
Ring toss with planets, it's all just a dare!
The Milky Way sings, a celestial band,
While gravity pulls us, we twirl hand in hand.

With laughter and fun wrapped in stardust so bright,
Join the cosmic carnival, a dazzling sight.
A galaxy's worth of joy in this show,
A night full of magic and endless glow!

Heavenly Hoedown

At the edge of the universe, we gather around,
For a good old hoedown on the cosmic ground.
With planets all polka dancing in line,
Each twirl and twist is a shimmering sign.

Shooting stars strum on their banjos so fine,
While meteors stomp, keeping perfect time.
The rings of Saturn provide a fine stage,
Where galaxies swing with joy and engage.

In this stellar barn, all are welcome to spin,
Cosmic critters laugh, let the fun begin!
With space hay bales and a comet for a pie,
We all sing together, our spirits fly high.

So grab a partner, let's dance through the skies,
In this heavenly hoedown, the laughter will rise.
Round up the stars and let merriment flow,
In a cosmic celebration, we steal the show!

Comet Capers

A comet zoomed past Earth one day,
With a tail that danced in a dazzling display.
It knocked off my hat in a wild, swirling spree,
And left me there speechless, oh who could it be?

The comet winked as it whizzed on by,
Chasing the moon, oh my, oh my!
It played a game of tag with Mars,
While kids on the ground wished on shooting stars!

Then off it zoomed, like a playful sprite,
Daring the planets to join in the flight.
Uranus laughed as it spun in place,
While Pluto just rolled, unable to race!

So remember the comet, dear friend of the night,
With giggles and sparks, it brought pure delight.
In the vastness above, it left quite a tale,
Of comets that caper and leave us all pale!

Milky Way Mirth

In the Milky Way, what a sight to see,
Stars throwing parties, all wild and free.
Jupiter's balloons and Saturn's cake,
A dance floor of rings, oh, for goodness' sake!

The aliens danced in their shiny attire,
Wobbling and laughing, oh, how they perspire!
They juggled asteroids, all round and gray,
Shouting 'Let's party', in a colorful way!

While Earthlings looked up, with eyes open wide,
Dreaming of cake for their sweet cosmic ride.
But the dance kept on, in the great starry glow,
As planets spun faster, putting on quite a show!

So if you look up, just peek in the night,
You might see a planet doing moonwalks in flight.
With giggles from stars and laughter from Mars,
The Milky Way's mirth shines brighter than ours!

Cosmic Comedy

In a universe vast, comedy reigns,
Black holes tell jokes that break all the chains.
Galaxies chuckle, colliding with glee,
While stars spin their tales of bright jubilee!

A neutron star winks, gives a cosmic grin,
Saying, 'Knock, knock! Who's there? Oh, come in!'
The space dust giggles, floats in the breeze,
As planets juggle meteors, aiming to please!

Comets wear glasses, just to look cool,
While asteroids do backflips, showing off their school.
They gather in clusters, rehearsing their skits,
As the universe cheers with rolling stone hits!

So here's to the funny, surreal and bright,
In the comedy cosmos where laughter takes flight.
From Jupiter's pranks to the sun's silly rays,
In this cosmic arena, hilarity plays!

Stellar Shenanigans

On a vibrant star, oh what a sight,
Aliens played hopscotch from day into night.
They used glowing asteroids for chalk on the ground,
With laughter and joy, their delight knows no bounds.

Venus wore boots that sparkled and shone,
While Mars cracked jokes, making everyone groan.
The moons had a race, all zipping around,
As comets cheered loudly, their tails trailing sound!

A nebula wobbled and spun like a top,
Gas clouds were brewing a fizzy pop shop.
They drank cosmic soda, fizzy and bright,
As black holes spun tales, pulling us tight!

So glance at the heavens, join in the fun,
Where stars play together under the sun.
With laughter and joy in the evening's embrace,
The universe giggles, a splendid place!

Stellar Smiles

Stars danced a jig in the night,
Planets played tag, what a sight!
Venus wore shades, looking quite cool,
While Mars laughed and acted the fool.

Jupiter boasted, 'I'm the biggest!'
While Saturn swayed with its ringed twists.
Neptune whispered, 'Don't make me pout!'
And Pluto threw a party, 'Come out!'

Comets zoomed by like they were late,
While asteroids rocked to a spacey fate.
Galileo grinned from a far-off seat,
As the Milky Way tapped to the beat.

Laughter echoed in the cosmic sea,
With starry beings feeling so free.
In this wild light year, they all agree,
Space is a playground for you and me!

Interstellar Indulgence

Well, here comes Mars with a candy stash,
Made of space rocks, oh what a crash!
He threw out gummies, a galactic treat,
Chasing around on his tiny feet.

Saturn spun round with treats in tow,
With rings of licorice putting on a show.
While Jupiter's moon played hopscotch above,
Dodging the things that the stars dream of.

Uranus, giggling with a playful prank,
Sprinkled some stardust in Pluto's tank.
The moons all snickered, what a grand mess,
Deep space parties, who'd dare to guess?

As comets flew by with winter's chill,
They offered hot cocoa to warm the thrill.
In galaxies far, who knows what will,
Bring laughter and joy, a cosmic skill!

Cosmic Caprice

In the vastness of space, all is quite cheeky,
Where meteors fall and the starlight is freaky.
Venus tried dancing, but tripped on a star,
While Mercury zoomed off, like, 'Hey, how bizarre!'

The orbits all giggled, a swirling ballet,
As planets engaged in a whimsical fray.
Neptune played peek-a-boo behind a bright sun,
While Saturn's rings jingled just for fun.

Out in the void, a black hole did yawn,
Sucked in some laughter, then spat out a dawn.
With cada bounce back, constellations would cheer,
As the universe spun, we all came near.

In galaxies packed with joyous delight,
Each cosmic being ignited the night.
With each twist and turn, we've all got our sights,
Set on the antics in these starry heights!

Astounding Asteroids

Asteroids gathered in a jolly parade,
Riding on solar winds, plans were laid.
They wore funky hats made of stardust and glee,
Chasing each other through space's free spree.

One asteroid spun like a top with great flair,
While others tumbled about without care.
'Hey, look at me!' one shouted with pride,
'The belt's just a dance floor, come join for a ride!'

They zipped past Mars, who looked rather shocked,
While Venus just giggled, her laughter unlocked.
They'd play leapfrog with moons, it was all quite a show,
In the asteroid belt, where fun would not slow.

So when you gaze up at the shimmering night,
Just remember the asteroids and their delight.
For in the cosmos, where wonders abound,
Every rock has a smile when friends are around!

Constellation Caprice

Oh, the stars gather round for a dance,
Twinkling with laughter, not a chance,
Orion trips over his own mighty bow,
While Cassiopeia shouts, "Look at me now!"

Pleiades giggling, they scatter and play,
While Draco complains he's lost a whole day,
With comets zooming, causing a stir,
They rattle the Milky Way without a blur!

The Big Dipper spills its drink with a splash,
As Vega points and says, "That's a big crash!"
Constellations chuckle, an endless jest,
In this cosmic carnival, they're simply the best!

Sunbeam Shenanigans

The sun wakes up with a mischievous grin,
Bouncing sunbeams, let the fun begin,
It tickles the planets, oh what a sight,
Mercury giggles, twirls with delight!

Venus, the diva, loves to show off,
Her rays dance around, making everyone scoff,
Earth joins in, planting silly pranks,
While Mars just mumbles, "Thanks for the thanks!"

Jupiter's storms brew a playful gale,
While Saturn spins rings for a big cosmic trail,
Uranus rolls over, quite out of control,
Laughing and jostling, it lightens our soul!

The Chaotic Cosmos

In the heavens where chaos reigns supreme,
Stars twist and twirl, living the dream,
Black holes giggle, making things disappear,
While meteors race, shouting, "We're here!"

Asteroids argue, who's the best rock,
While comets critique, "You really do cock!"
Gravity grapples, pulling all tight,
As Saturn just chuckles, "What a sight!"

Galaxies swirl in a wacky parade,
With supernovae bursts, a grand escapade,
The universe twinkles with smiles every day,
In this chaotic dance, let's frolic and play!

Planetary Parodies

Mercury whispers, "I'm the fastest around!"
But Venus winks, "I've got beauty unbound!"
Earth rolls her eyes, "What's all this fuss?"
While Mars just scoffs, "Aren't you all thus?"

Jupiter grins, "I've got the most moons!"
And Saturn chimes in, "I spin with tunes!"
Uranus just laughs, "You all make me giggle,
My tilt's so unique, I truly wiggle!"

Neptune, the elder, nods with a sigh,
"You all are so silly, don't ever be shy!"
As the planets perform their comedy show,
In this playful realm, they steal the whole glow!

Whirlpool of Whimsy

In a galaxy far, stars danced in glee,
Pluto played tag with a comet or three.
Venus wore shades, but forgot to blend,
While Mars challenged Jupiter to a long bend.

Saturn's rings sparkled, not a care in sight,
While Neptune giggled, sparkling with light.
Mercury zoomed in a frantic race,
But tripped on an asteroid, what a grimace!

Uranus spun round with a chuckle and cheer,
While Earth just shrugged, drinking root beer.
Galactic goof-ups gave everyone chuckles,
As the stars sent messages filled with big snuggles.

So if you look up at night, take a glance,
In this wacky whirlpool, the stars love to dance.
With laughter and smiles in cosmic delight,
Join the fun, let your worries take flight.

Stellar Slip-ups

The sun told a joke that only it knew,
But Mercury shrugged, adjusting its hue.
Venus spilled coffee on the Milky Way,
As Jupiter laughed, brightening the day.

Saturn tried hula-hooping, lost all its rings,
While Mars painted murals of whimsical things.
Neptune got dizzy on a ride of its own,
While comets whizzed by, making merry and moan.

Uranus rolled over, quite tickled and bold,
As Earth tried to join in, a sight to behold.
A slip on a meteoroid led to a tumble,
And the laughter erupted, a humorous jumble.

In this stellar space of odd little quirks,
Galactic shenanigans, where nobody lurks,
So peek at the skies, with a smile that won't stop,
And find the fun under every star's hop!

Quasar Quirks

There once lived a quasar, shiny and bright,
Trying to twirl with all of its might.
But it spun so fast, it lost a few rays,
While the others just giggled, "Is this how you play?"

A black hole yawned, about to steal dreams,
But starlight bounced back with mischievous beams.
A supernova sneezed, and scattered confetti,
While silly old planets felt rather unsteady.

Galaxy children chased light like a kite,
Playing catch with a neutron star, oh what a sight!
Orbits got tangled, a cosmic ballet,
And even the dark matter couldn't help but sway.

So next time you gaze at the night's twinkly tricks,
Remember the laughter in all of the flicks.
From quasars to black holes, the universe sings,
With quirks and with giggles, oh what joy it brings!

Meteorite Mayhem

A meteor sped by with a winky eye,
Telling the stars, "I'm too cool to fly!"
But whoops, it got stuck in a comet's long tail,
Creating a chaos that was sure to derail.

Earth threw a party, with cakes made of dust,
While moons had a dance that turned quite robust.
Mercury twirled but forgot to rehearse,
Landing smack-dab in the middle of verse.

The stars all united, in laughter and fun,
As they created their own meteor run.
Uranus threw glitter that sparkled so bright,
While Venus cheered loudly, "This feels just right!"

So up in the cosmos, where silliness reigns,
The antics continue despite all the strains.
So chase after laughter, let worries decline,
In the realm of the meteors, joy is divine!

Nebulae Noodles

In a swirl of clouds, they dance and twirl,
Pasta shapes floating and making us whirl.
Spaghetti comets zoom past the sun,
While meatball meteorites join in the fun.

Sauce spills like stardust on a cosmic plate,
Jupiter serves up garlic—oh, isn't that great?
Mars rolls around with a cheesy grin,
As Saturn slurps noodles without a din.

Nebula chefs stir in the spacey delight,
Creating a feast that's out of sight.
A cosmic dinner, oh what a sight,
With stars twinkling down like they're feeling polite.

So grab a fork, take a bite, just be bold,
In this cosmic kitchen, the magic unfolds.
Here in the void, everybody's invited,
For a noodle party that's truly excited!

Antics at Alpha Centauri

At Alpha Centauri, the aliens play,
With three-legged races, cheering all day.
One juggling moons, another spins rings,
Laughter erupts as the universe sings.

A wormhole slide takes them for a spin,
While comets collide with a laugh and a grin.
Chasing black holes, they tumble and roll,
Echoes of giggles through space they extol.

Martian mates join with their pranks on the run,
While Venus shines down with a luminescent fun.
Galactic clowns paint weird faces afar,
In this stellar circus, they're all shining stars.

The space-time bends as they dance in delight,
Creating wild memories under the night.
With friendships that stretch across the whole sky,
At Alpha Centauri, the laughter runs high!

Starship Shenanigans

In a starship built from bubblegum dreams,
They blast through the cosmos with whimsical beams.
Control panels spark, making silly sounds,
As they zoom through the orbits and roundabouts found.

With a whoosh and a phew, they take off in glee,
Chasing light beams and pretending to flee.
Zipping past planets, they make goofy faces,
As they race with the comets in cosmic embraces.

The pilot spills juice on the captain's bright hat,
While asteroids laugh as they scatter and chat.
Galaxies swirl with a chuckle or two,
As they navigate nebulae, giggling anew.

So buckle up tight for an interstellar ride,
With starship shenanigans, there's nowhere to hide.
Each loop-de-loop brings another round of cheer,
In this cosmic caper, the fun's always near!

Quirky Quasars

Quasars are flickering with zany delight,
Their beams spin around like a crazy kite.
One wears a tutu, another a hat,
As they waltz through the void, just imagine that!

A galactic party where everyone glows,
Twirling and jumping, in gravity flows.
With music from pulsars—the beat never stops,
As quizzical questions from stardust pops.

Playing hopscotch on the milky way's edge,
Daring black holes with hilarious pledge.
Slinky starlight wraps their cosmic parade,
In a mischievous game that won't ever fade.

So join in the laughter where cosmic winds blow,
With quirky quasars putting on a show.
For in this universe, joy fills every crack,
As they dance through the galaxies, never look back!

Jovial Journey through the Stars

A comet with a silly grin,
Zooms past Mars, just for a spin.
Venus giggles, doing a twirl,
As Saturn's rings begin to whirl.

The sun winks brightly, full of cheer,
While asteroids dance, no need to steer.
Jupiter jumps, with a side-to-side,
Pluto chuckles, not one to hide.

Neptune hums a joyful tune,
As stars sparkle like balloons.
Galaxies spin, all full of glee,
In this cosmic jamboree!

So come along, let's take a ride,
Across the cosmos, side by side.
With laughter echoing, oh so bright,
Join this playful, starry night!

Cosmic Whims

There's a meteor with a quirky cap,
Flipping and flopping, what a mishap!
Mercury darts with a cheeky grin,
While clouds on Neptune just laugh and spin.

Uranus chuckles, 'Oh, what a sight!'
As comets make a slapstick flight.
Mars tries to juggle, but oh dear me,
He fumbles and tumbles, can't you see?

Stars are snickering, twinkling in glee,
As aliens dance in zero gravity.
A black hole burps, what a strange show,
Making everyone laugh, oh so slow!

The moon cartwheels in a shimmering gown,
While Saturn's rings go up and down.
A cosmic party, wild and free,
Join this frolic, come twirl with me!

Planets in Play

Pluto plays hide and seek at night,
While Mars juggles rocks with delight.
Earth throws a party, all are invited,
Around the stars, the fun excited!

Venus whispers a joke to the sun,
Who chuckles warmly, 'Oh, what fun!'
Neptune joins in with a gleeful shout,
As Mercury zooms in, quick and sprout.

Jupiter claps with thunderous glee,
While Saturn shows off with a grand spree.
Asteroids tumble, making us laugh,
In this playful cosmic photograph.

Galaxies swirl in a dizzy dance,
As comets zoom by in a playful trance.
The night sky sparkles, joy on display,
In this merry cosmos, come join the play!

Laughter across the Cosmos

Shooting stars giggle, racing their friends,
As they zip through space, making amends.
The sun plays tag, light flickering fast,
While planets cheer on, having a blast.

Black holes make faces with delightful flair,
While tiny moons perform in thin air.
Venus brags of her beauty so bright,
But Mars rolls his eyes, 'What a sight!'

Jupiter boasts of his swirling storms,
While Saturn spins in fantastic forms.
Neptune sings salty songs of the sea,
As we laugh together, wild and free.

In the vastness, don't be shy,
Join the fun; oh me, oh my!
Together we'll dance through this endless space,
Spreading joy and laughter all over the place!

Cosmic Capers

A comet zooms by with a tail so bright,
It tickles the stars, what a comical sight!
Planets play hide and seek in the night,
While asteroids dance with pure delight.

Saturn spins rings just to show off his bling,
While Mars brags loudly, 'I'm the best thing!'
Venus, the diva, gives a twirl with flair,
Jupiter chuckles, 'Look at my hair!'

Interplanetary Intrigues

Uranus spins sideways, oh what a tease,
While Neptune keeps swirling like a cool breeze.
Earth rolls its eyes, 'What a weird parade!'
The moons all giggle, 'Not one home's made!'

Mercury zips by, a blitz in a rush,
With Venus behind him, oh what a hush!
They play bumper cars in the cosmic lanes,
While stardust laughs echo in playful chains.

Galactic Guffaws

A black hole sneezes, 'Ah-choo!' oh dear,
Swallowing stars, brings giggles and cheer.
A wayward space probe yells, 'What's our fate?'
But the satellites tease, 'We're never late!'

The Sun tells a joke, but no one can hear,
Because light travels slow and they're all out here.
Pluto rolls laughing, amidst all the laughs,
Declaring, 'Why not? I'm still in the graphs!'

Starry Shenanigans

In a nebula's mist, where the wild things roam,
Aliens pluck planets to decorate their dome.
A shooting star wishes for free ice cream,
While meteor showers join in the gleam.

Jupiter's stormy dance has everyone stunned,
While Venus serves snacks, oh what fun is spun!
Galaxies giggle at their cosmic games,
As the universe chuckles, calling all names.

Interstellar Improv

A comet cracked a joke one day,
It zoomed past Earth in a playful way.
The stars all giggled, twinkled with glee,
As planets joined in for a cosmic spree.

Mars wore a hat, quite floppy and round,
While Venus danced, making silly sounds.
The moons flopped about in a wild ballet,
Creating laughter in the Milky Way.

Jupiter chuckled with clouds in a swirl,
As Saturn's rings began to twirl.
Uranus joked, "I'm the funniest dude!"
While Neptune blushed, feeling quite lewd.

With interstellar antics all in a row,
They played tag with asteroids, stealing the show.
In the vastness of space, they made a grand scene,
Of cosmic mischief, so bright and serene.

Celestial Clowning

On the edge of a nebula, bright and bold,
Jovial giants gathered, their stories told.
One moon pulled a prank, made a big splash,
While the sun burst out with a dazzling flash.

Earth wore a pie on its wobbly head,
As laughter echoed from everything spread.
The aliens watched, oh what a delight!
In the vastness of space, all was just right.

Pluto sat chuckling, the smallest of all,
Said, "I'll bring humor to this cosmic ball!"
With asteroid acrobatics and some stellar cheer,
Clowning around brought them all near.

Galaxies spun, their dance full of flair,
Tickling comets, giggles full of air.
In this vast expanse, nothing felt grim,
As merriment flowed like a playful whim.

Galactic Goofiness

In a universe wide, where the laughter flows,
Galaxies bumbled, playing tag like pros.
A black hole spun, sent a star flying,
With goofy grins, there was no denying.

Saturn's rings danced, a geometric jest,
While the sun wore sunglasses, looking its best.
"Who's the brightest?" quipped sneaky old Mars,
As the moons laughed and played among the stars.

Mercury zipped, trying hard not to fall,
With a quick little twirl, he excited them all.
Neptune splashed in with a bubbly glee,
Galactic goofiness was wild and carefree.

With each cosmic caper, joy burst in waves,
As planets and comets spun through the graves.
Clowns of the cosmos embraced the sheer fun,
Creating a symphony under the sun.

Nebulous Nonsense

In a puff of cloud, where the stardust twirls,
The planets engaged in some silly swirls.
Asteroids chased comets in a dizzying race,
While aliens juggled in spirals of space.

A star took a tumble, laughed loud and bright,
As the sun shouted, "Hey! That's quite a sight!"
Moonbeams were bouncy, so light and spry,
While the gas giants giggled and watched from on high.

"Let's spin some tales of twinkling delight!"
Cried Venus to Mercury, "Come join the plight!"
The nebulae winked in vibrant array,
Sharing memories of absurd things that play.

With quirky antics and laughter galore,
The cosmos embraced its whimsical core.
In this nebula filled with laughter and glee,
The universe shone, oh so playfully free!

www.ingramcontent.com/pod-product-compliance
Lightning Source LLC
Chambersburg PA
CBHW071836160426
43209CB00003B/322